D1709486

"That sweet Hay, Whereon the blessed Babie lay".—Herrick.

When Jesus Christ was born (the legend saith)
The fodder, dried and brown, whereon He lay,
Knew its Creator, and awoke from death
To greet the Lord of Life that happy day.
For Him no royal coverlet was spread,
But rose-pink Sainfoin blossomed round His head,-
The asses' fodder turned to Holy Hay.

Cicely Mary Barker

Cover Design and Family Tree Illustration
by Anita M. Meyer

ISBN 0-937739-13-8   Printed and Bound in U.S.A.

Our Family's Christmas Memories

CHRISTMAS

"HEAVEN AND EARTH, THROUGH THE SPOTLESS BIRTH,
ARE AT PEACE ON THIS NIGHT SO FAIR."

featuring the art
of

Cicely Mary Barker

Published
by

Roman, Inc.   Roselle, Il 60172

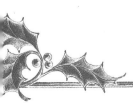

About Cicely Mary Barker

Born in the twilight of the Victorian era in Croydon in the south of England, Cicely Mary Barker became a world renowned artist beloved by children and adults alike.

A frail, delicate child, a victim of epilepsy, she found creative outlets at an early age to compensate for her physical limitations.

Her sensitivity for children, animals, the delicacy of flowers and her abiding Christian faith are manifest in her body of paintings, cards, illustrations, church panels and stained glass windows.

Noted initially for her delightful series, "The Flower Fairies", which became children's classics she progressed to penetrating religious themes. These works reveal her genuine compassion for people and her reverence for things spiritual.

Cicely Mary Barker lived until 1973 and worked almost until the end. Her life spanned many decades of dramatically different social cultures. The constancy of her artistic message prevails even today and no doubt will live to touch future generations.

The Christ-child stood at Mary's knee,
His hair was like a crown,
And all the flowers looked up at Him,
And all the stars looked down.

G.K Chesterton

THE STRANGER~GUEST.

WHOSO SHALL RECEIVE ONE SUCH LITTLE CHILD IN MY NAME,
RECEIVETH ME.

Thanksgivings to Remember

Date_____

On Thanksgiving Day we_____
_____
_____

Thanksgiving Dinner was_____
_____

We are thankful for_____
_____
_____

Date_____

On Thanksgiving Day we_____
_____

Thanksgiving Dinner was_____
_____

We are thankful for_____
_____

Date_____

On Thanksgiving Day we_____
_____

Thanksgiving Dinner was_____
_____

We are thankful for_____
_____

O give thanks unto the Lord
for He is good, and His mercy
endures forever.

Psalm 106:1

Thanksgivings to Remember

Date _____

On Thanksgiving Day we _____

_____

_____

Thanksgiving Dinner was _____

_____

We are thankful for _____

_____

_____

Date _____

On Thanksgiving Day we _____

_____

_____

Thanksgiving Dinner was _____

_____

We are thankful for _____

_____

_____

Date _____

On Thanksgiving Day we _____

_____

_____

Thanksgiving Dinner was _____

_____

We are thankful for _____

_____

Our Holiday Guests

Signature	Date		Signature	Date

WITH ANGELS AND
ARCHANGELS, AND
WITH ALL THE

COMPANY OF HEAVEN,
WE LAUD AND MAGNIFY
THY GLORIOUS NAME.

Our Holiday Guests

Signature   Date   Signature   Date   Signature   Date

_____ _____ _____ _____ _____ _____

_____ _____ _____ _____ _____ _____

_____ _____ _____ _____ _____ _____

_____ _____ _____ _____ _____ _____

_____ _____ _____ _____ _____ _____

_____ _____ _____ _____ _____ _____

_____ _____ _____ _____ _____ _____

_____ _____ _____ _____ _____ _____

_____ _____ _____ _____ _____ _____

_____ _____ _____ _____ _____ _____

_____ _____ _____ _____ _____ _____

_____ _____ _____ _____ _____ _____

_____ _____ _____ _____ _____ _____

_____ _____ _____ _____ _____ _____

_____ _____ _____ _____ _____ _____

_____ _____ _____ _____ _____ _____

_____ _____ _____ _____ _____ _____

_____ _____ _____ _____ _____ _____

_____ _____ _____ _____ _____ _____

_____ _____ _____ _____ _____ _____

_____ _____ _____ _____ _____ _____

_____ _____ _____ _____ _____ _____

_____ _____ _____ _____ _____ _____

CHRISTMAS

·UNTO·US·A·CHILD·IS·
·BORN·

Christmas Memories

Year_____

Christmas Eve _____

_____

_____

Christmas Day _____

_____

_____

Christmas Dinner was _____

_____

Year_____

Christmas Eve _____

_____

_____

Christmas Day _____

_____

_____

Christmas Dinner was _____

_____

Year_____

Christmas Eve _____

_____

_____

Christmas Day _____

_____

_____

Christmas Dinner was _____

_____

BETHLEHEM ≈ THE HOUSE OF BREAD.

I AM THE LIVING BREAD WHICH CAME DOWN FROM HEAVEN ~

For to us a child is born,
to us a Son is given

Isaiah 9:6

Christmas Memories

Year _____

Christmas Eve _____
_____

Christmas Day _____
_____

Christmas Dinner was _____
_____

Year _____

Christmas Eve _____
_____

Christmas Day _____
_____

Christmas Dinner was _____
_____

Year _____

Christmas Eve _____
_____

Christmas Day _____
_____

Christmas Dinner was _____
_____

O Tannenbaum

Place photos of family
in front of Christmas tree here.

O Tannenbaum

Place photos of family
in front of Christmas tree here.

EMMANUEL — GOD WITH US.

O holy Infant, small and dear,
Your birthday once again is here,
And joyful songs ring near and far
Wherever little children are.

Anonymous

Christmas Celebrations

Date _____

Event _____

Place _____

_____

_____

Place
Photo
Here

Place
Photo
Here

Date _____

Event _____

Place _____

_____

_____

INASMUCH AS·YE·HAVE ·DONE·IT· UNTO·ONE· OF·THE·

LEAST· OF·THESE· YE·HAVE· DONE·IT· UNTO·ME.

Lovely Lady dressed in blue, Teach me how to pray.
God was just your little boy and you know the way.

Mary Dixon Thayer

Our Family Traditions

What _____

_____

When it started _____

What _____

_____

When it started _____

What _____

_____

When it started _____

What _____

_____

When it started _____

What _____

_____

When it started _____

What _____

_____

When it started _____

What _____

_____

When it started _____

What _____

_____

When it started _____

What _____

_____

When it started _____

What _____

_____

When it started _____

What _____

_____

When it started _____

What _____

_____

When it started _____

...and He shall be called the
Prince of Peace.

Isaiah 9:6

Our Family Members

Name   Relationship

Our Family Tree

Place Mother's Picture Here

Place Maternal Grandmother's Picture Here

Place Maternal Grandfather's Picture Here

PARENTS

GRANDPARENTS

Place Father's Picture Here

Place Paternal Grandfather's Picture Here

Place Paternal Grandmother's Picture Here

CHILDREN

Place
First Born's
Picture
Here

ANITA M. MEYER

IF I HAD LIVED IN BETHLEHEM

If I had lived in Bethlehem that far-off Christmas Day,
And knelt before the manger-bed where Mary's Baby lay,
     Would that dear Mother, do you think, have granted me the joy
     Of holding Him, as now I hold our neighbour's baby boy?

O carefully, O tenderly, if I were trusted so,
Should I have rocked my tiny Lord those many years ago!
Yet even now, it almost seems this very babe is He,
The little Jesus in my arms, by Mary lent to me.

Cicley Mary Barker

Additions to Our Family

Name————————————————

Date————————————————

Place of Birth————————————

————————————————

————————————————

Place
Photo
Here

Place
Photo
Here

Name————————————————

Date————————————————

Place of Birth————————————

————————————————

————————————————

Every good and perfect gift
is from above.

James 1:17

Special Gifts

Date _____

To _____

From _____

Gift was _____

_____

Date _____

To _____

From _____

Gift was _____

_____

Date _____

To _____

From _____

Gift was _____

_____

Date _____

To _____

From _____

Gift was _____

_____

Date _____

To _____

From _____

Gift was _____

_____

Date _____

To _____

From _____

Gift was _____

_____

Date _____

To _____

From _____

Gift was _____

_____

Date _____

To _____

From _____

Gift was _____

_____

Date _____

To _____

From _____

Gift was _____

_____

Date _____

To _____

From _____

Gift was _____

_____

Mary took her Baby, she dressed Him so sweet

Special Gifts

Photo to the right is _____

Gift was _____

From _____

Date _____

Place photo here
of loved one
opening gift

Place photo here
of loved one
opening gift

Photo to the left is:

_____

Gift was _____

_____

From _____

Date _____

Shout for joy to the Lord
all the earth.

Psalm 100:1

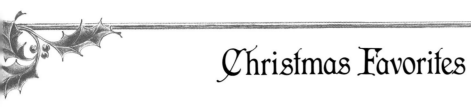

Christmas Favorites

Carols

Stories

Movies

Photos & Mementos

Family Feasts
Photo Page

Traditional Holiday Recipes

Recipe _____   Directions _____
Ingredients:
                                   _____
                                   _____
                                   _____
                                   _____
                                   _____
                                   _____
                                   _____
                                   _____
                                   _____
                                   _____
                                   _____

                                   Rating ★ ★ ★ ★ ★   Serves _____

Recipe _____   Directions _____
Ingredients:
                                   _____
                                   _____
                                   _____
                                   _____
                                   _____
                                   _____
                                   _____
                                   _____
                                   _____
                                   _____
                                   _____

                                   Rating ★ ★ ★ ★ ★   Serves _____

Recipe _____   Directions _____
Ingredients:
                                   _____
                                   _____
                                   _____
                                   _____
                                   _____
                                   _____
                                   _____
                                   _____
                                   _____

                                   Rating ★ ★ ★ ★ ★   Serves _____

Traditional Holiday Recipes

Recipe _____

Ingredients:

Directions_____
_____
_____
_____
_____
_____
_____
_____
_____
_____
_____
_____

Rating ★ ★ ★ ★ ★   Serves _____

Recipe _____

Ingredients:

Directions_____
_____
_____
_____
_____
_____
_____
_____
_____
_____
_____
_____

Rating ★ ★ ★ ★ ★   Serves _____

Recipe _____

Ingredients:

Directions_____
_____
_____
_____
_____
_____
_____
_____
_____
_____
_____
_____

Rating ★ ★ ★ ★ ★   Serves _____

Our Family's New Year's Resolutions

Year _____

Our biggest news of the year _____

Our Family's resolutions for the new year _____

_____

Year _____

Our biggest news of the year _____

Our Family's resolutions for the new year _____

_____

Year _____

Our biggest news of the year _____

Our Family's resolutions for the new year _____

_____

Year _____

Our biggest news of the year _____

Our Family's resolutions for the new year _____

_____

Year _____

Our biggest news of the year _____

Our Family's resolutions for the new year _____

_____

Year _____

Our biggest news of the year _____

Our Family's resolutions for the new year _____

_____

TO GUIDE OUR FEET
INTO THE WAY OF
PEACE